Leap and Dance

The lion walks on padded paws,
The squirrel leaps from limb to limb,
While flies can crawl straight up a wall,
And seals can dive and swim.
The worm, it wiggles all around,
The monkey swings by its tail,
And birds may hop upon the ground,
Or spread their wings and sail.
But boys and girls have much more fun;
 They leap and dance
 And walk
 And *run*.

Anonymous

Little People™ Big Book

About
THE ANIMAL KINGDOM

TIME LIFE for Children™

ALEXANDRIA, VIRGINIA

Table of Contents

ANIMALS ARE AMAZING

ANIMALS DO SURPRISING THINGS

ANIMALS BUILD INCREDIBLE HOMES

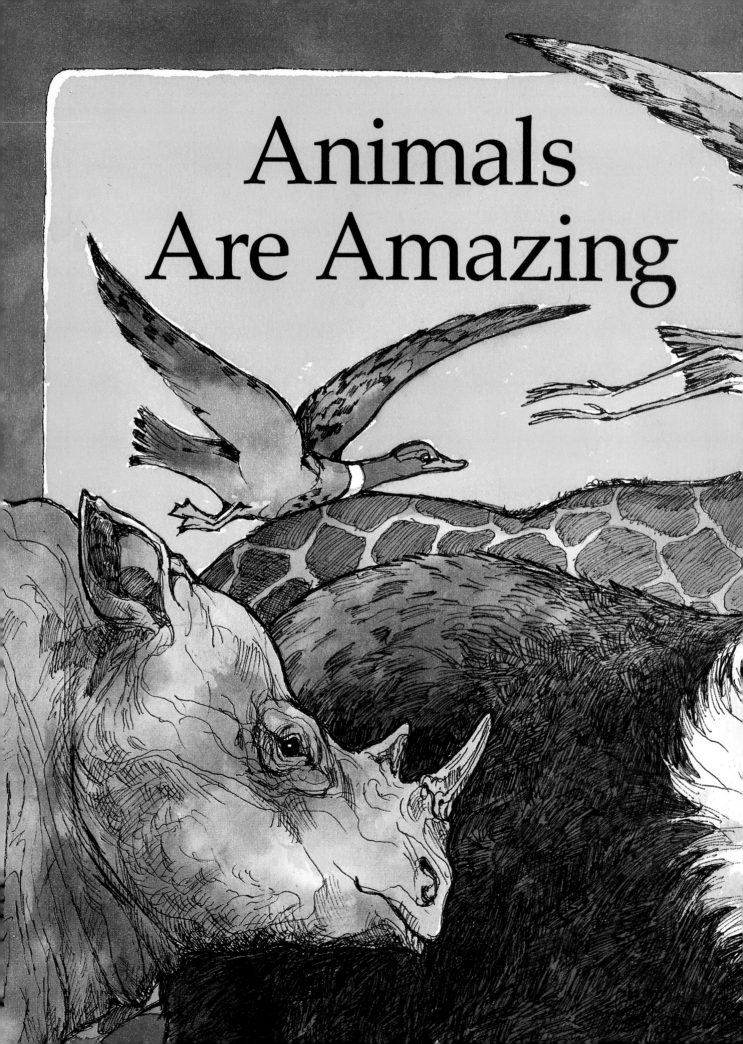

Animals
Are Amazing

Words and Pictures

The 🦏 has a horn, and the 🐟 has a gill;

The 🦒 has a hoof, and the 🦆 has a bill;

The 🐦 has a wing, that on high it may sail;

And the 🐻 has a paw, and the 🐿 has a tail;

And they swim, or they fly, or they walk, or they soar,

With fin, or with wing, or with feet, two or four.

Traditional

MARVELOUS MAMMALS

Mammals are not like any other animals in the world. Their body temperature stays about the same whether the weather is cold or hot. They all breathe air—even the mammals that live in water. All of them have some fur or hair on their bodies at some time during their lives. And, most important, the mammal mother produces milk in her body to feed her babies. Usually, the baby—or babies—grow inside the body of the mother.

KANGAROO mothers have pouches that their tiny babies climb into. The babies stay there while they grow bigger. Kangaroos are champion jumpers. With their strong hind legs, they can make jumps of 25 feet or more. They are also fast runners. In a race between a kangaroo and a racehorse, the kangaroo would win! Kangaroos live in Australia or on neighboring islands.

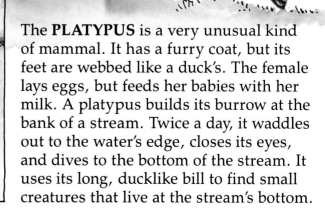

The **PLATYPUS** is a very unusual kind of mammal. It has a furry coat, but its feet are webbed like a duck's. The female lays eggs, but feeds her babies with her milk. A platypus builds its burrow at the bank of a stream. Twice a day, it waddles out to the water's edge, closes its eyes, and dives to the bottom of the stream. It uses its long, ducklike bill to find small creatures that live at the stream's bottom.

A CAMEL is easy to recognize. It always has either one or two humps in its back. The camel is a desert animal, so it often has to go without food or water. It stores fat in the hump for the days when it has nothing to eat. When food is scarce, the hump gets smaller. When there is plenty of food, it grows bigger again.

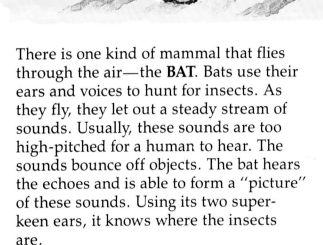

There is one kind of mammal that flies through the air—the **BAT**. Bats use their ears and voices to hunt for insects. As they fly, they let out a steady stream of sounds. Usually, these sounds are too high-pitched for a human to hear. The sounds bounce off objects. The bat hears the echoes and is able to form a ''picture'' of these sounds. Using its two super-keen ears, it knows where the insects are.

A **DOLPHIN** is a mammal that spends its whole life in the water. Dolphins swim in groups called ''schools'' and give off high-pitched sounds like bats do. These sounds bounce off objects in the water, telling the dolphin if it is likely to hit anything. A dolphin can stay underwater for about five minutes. Then it has to surface for air. It breathes through nostrils located in a blowhole on the top of its head. Dolphins are very intelligent, and they like people.

7

MEET SOME FANTASTIC FISH

Fish are animals that spend their lives in the water. They breathe through gills instead of lungs. They have fins for swimming instead of legs for walking. Fish are cold-blooded. Their temperature changes according to the temperature of the water around them. They usually have bony skeletons and scales to protect their bodies.

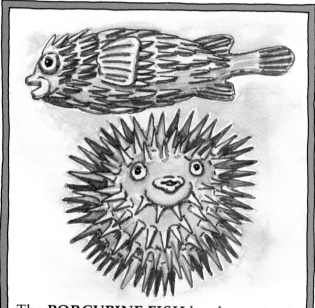

The **PORCUPINE FISH** has long, stout spines that stick out in every direction. When threatened, it can take in extra air or water and blow itself up into a puffy ball three times its normal size. The spines make these fish hard to handle and dangerous to other fish.

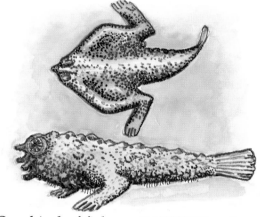

One kind of fish—a **BATFISH**—doesn't swim. Its fins are not really fins. They are more like legs. The batfish uses them to walk around. This fish is quite small (from 8 to 12 inches long) and lives in warm waters. When you look down at it from above, it looks like a bat.

The **AFRICAN LUNGFISH** is a most unusual fish. It has lungs just like a land animal. In very hot weather, when shallow pools of water dry up, the lungfish wriggles deep into the mud. Then it folds its body in half and prepares a kind of moist cocoon. A tiny hole at the top lets in air. The lungfish may sleep for as long as five years, waiting until flood waters come again to soften the cocoon. When the waters come, the lungfish wakes up.

8

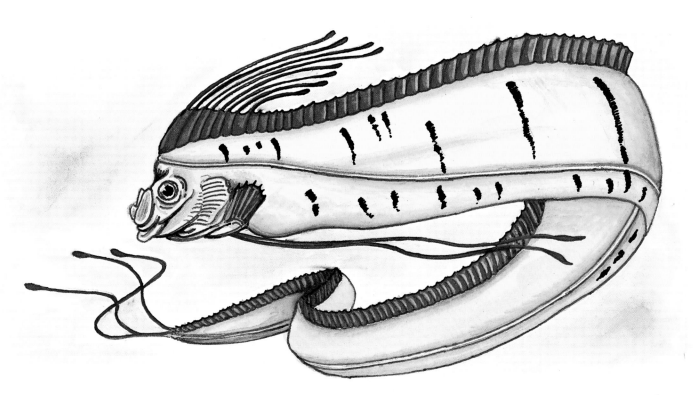

The **OARFISH** is a ribbonlike fish that can grow as long as 49 feet. Bright red spines stick out from its head. This fish looks quite frightening, but it is really harmless. When people think they have seen a sea monster, they may have been looking at an oarfish.

The **HAMMERHEAD SHARK** has a head shaped just like a hammer's head. There is a nostril at each end of the "hammer." When this shark smells its prey, it swings its head from side to side. The hammerhead may grow over 12 feet long and weigh 1,000 pounds.

THE FABULOUS FLIERS

Birds are animals with feathers. All of them have wings, though a few of them cannot fly. Like mammals, birds have backbones and are warm-blooded. They have beaks instead of jaws, and they lay eggs—usually in nests.

BLACK SKIMMERS are birds that don't build a real nest. They scrape out a very shallow hole in which to lay their eggs. They prefer an island beach or a sandbar surrounded on three sides by water. The lower half of the skimmer's beak is much longer than the top half. The skimmer lets its lower bill trail through the water as it flies. When the bill finds a fish, the skimmer closes its beak and lifts the fish out of the water.

BOWERBIRDS are truly amazing! At courting time the males build fancy platforms of sticks and grass and ferns. Overhead, they hang vines, bamboo branches, and long grasses to make an arched roof, or "bower." They also decorate the area with leaves, flowers, beetle wings, and shells. When the flowers and leaves wither, the birds replace them with fresh ones. They use the "stage" to perform little dances and parade before the female.

The **CUCKOO** mother doesn't build her own nest. She just goes around to other nests while the mothers are away getting food. The cuckoo lifts out an egg and either eats it or drops it on the ground. Then she lays an egg of her own in the other mother's nest. She may lay as many as 12 eggs, each one in the nest of a different mother bird, who will raise the cuckoo chick as her own. She picks birds whose eggs look like her own. This kind of cuckoo lives mostly in Europe and Asia. The kind that lives in America usually builds its own nests.

The **AFRICAN GRAY PARROT** can imitate almost any sound. It has been known to learn as many as 500 words. It can also repeat songs perfectly and mimic creaking doors and barking dogs. Of course when these parrots talk, they don't understand what they are saying. In wild jungle forests, they only shriek and squawk. There are no humans around for them to imitate.

The **KIWI** is a bird that can't fly. It has no tail, and its wings are only 2 inches long. During the day it rolls up in a little ball and sleeps in burrows or small caves. At night it comes out of its hiding place to hunt for worms, spiders, and beetles with its long, sharp beak. The kiwi has a very good sense of smell. Its nostrils are located at the tip of its long beak.

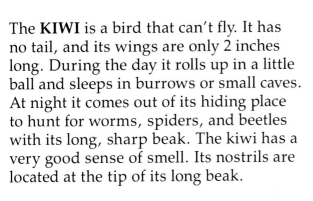

11

REMARKABLE REPTILES

Snakes, lizards, turtles, and alligators are all reptiles. (So were dinosaurs!) They are cold-blooded animals—like fish. Reptiles crawl on the ground, though some prefer to swim. They have tough, scaly skin, and most of them lay leathery-shelled eggs.

The Eastern Diamondback **RATTLESNAKE** is very dangerous. Snakes can feel vibrations in the ground when another animal moves. When the rattlesnake senses that its prey is near, it glides swiftly forward and sinks its poisonous fangs into the victim. If a large animal (or person) comes close, the snake shakes a rattle at the end of its tail. This warns the enemy not to come any closer. The rattle is made up of a group of hollow shells of dry skin. Each time the snake sheds its skin—at least once a year—it adds a new piece to the rattle.

The **ANACONDA** is the world's largest snake. It can grow as long as a school bus. These giant snakes are usually found where there is water. They hide near the banks of streams and swamps, waiting until an animal comes for a drink. Then, with a quick, looping motion, an anaconda wraps itself around the animal's body, squeezing out the air. It can swallow its prey whole because its jaws are loosely joined together. This allows its mouth to open very wide.

12

The **KOMODO DRAGON** is the biggest living lizard in the world. It can grow to a length of 10 feet—a little longer than most cows. It often weighs as much as 300 pounds. It hunts deer, wild pigs, monkeys, and even calves, and it is supposed to be very bad-tempered. It lives only on islands north of Australia.

Perhaps because **TUATARAS** have existed for more than 150 million years, they seem to do everything in slow motion. They take about ten breaths an hour. They chew their food for a long time. And their eggs take more than a year to hatch. On a tuatara's head there is a small spot very much like a third eye. This "blind eye" doesn't see, but it does seem to detect light. The tuatara grows to a length of only 2 to 2½ feet.

Turtles carry their houses with them in the form of a thick, heavy shell. The **ALLIGATOR SNAPPING TURTLE** is the largest fresh-water turtle. It lies on the muddy bottom of a pond, opens its huge mouth, and wiggles its pink, wormlike tongue. Fish spot the wriggling tongue and swim toward it, thinking they are going to get a fresh juicy worm for dinner. Snap! go the turtle's powerful jaws. A snapping turtle can be dangerous.

13

The Yak

Yickity-yackity, yickity-yak,
the yak has a scriffily, scraffily back;
some yaks are brown yaks and some yaks are black,
yickity-yackity, yickity-yak.

Sniggildy-snaggildy, sniggildy-snag,
the yak is all covered with shiggildy-shag;
he walks with a ziggildy-zaggildy-zag,
sniggildy-snaggildy, sniggildy-snag.

Yickity-yackity, yickity-yak,
the yak has a scriffily, scraffily back;
some yaks are brown and some yaks are black,
yickity-yackity, yickity-yak.

Jack Prelutsky

14

Elephant

The elephant's a bulky beast;
He weighs a thousand pounds at least;
And what to you would be a feast
   Is not a filler-upper
To him. All day he has to hunch
Above his trough and munch and munch
And by the time he's done with lunch
It's time to start on supper.

Mary Ann Hoberman

The Ostrich Is a Silly Bird

The ostrich is a silly bird
   With scarcely any mind.
He often runs so very fast
   He leaves himself behind.

Mary E. Wilkins Freeman

15

WHO'S THE FASTEST?
WHO'S THE SLOWEST?

There are two birds that can break speed records. The *PEREGRINE FALCON*—flying high above the ground—can dive at a speed of 175 miles per hour. *SPINE-TAILED SWIFTS* can go as fast as 100 miles an hour when flying straight ahead. Their short legs are weak, however. They can hardly walk!

The *CHEETAH*, a kind of wild cat, is the fastest land animal. It can sprint up to 70 miles an hour for short distances. (A human is going fast if he or she runs at a speed of 15 miles per hour.) Cheetahs are amazing because they can reach full speed in just 2 seconds—faster than a racing car.

The fastest fish is the *SAILFISH*. It has been clocked at a speed of 68 miles per hour. The sailfish has a great fin on its back that it can raise above the water to catch the wind like a sail. When not in use, the fin folds back into a groove on the upper part of its body. Sailfish are about 20 feet long and can weigh as much as 1,000 pounds.

A *PRONGHORN ANTELOPE* can run at speeds of 50 miles an hour. It can go for long distances because it has well-developed lungs and its heart is about twice as big as those of other animals the same size.

The slowest mammal is the *THREE-TOED SLOTH*. It hangs upside down in trees and sleeps about 18 hours a day. The rest of the time it spends eating. On the ground it can go about 8 feet a minute, but it usually prefers not to move at all.

The *SNAIL* is the slowest animal of all. It would take a wood snail a half-day to travel the length of a football field. It has only one foot and carries its shell on its back. You probably wouldn't move very fast either if you had just one foot and carried your house on your back!

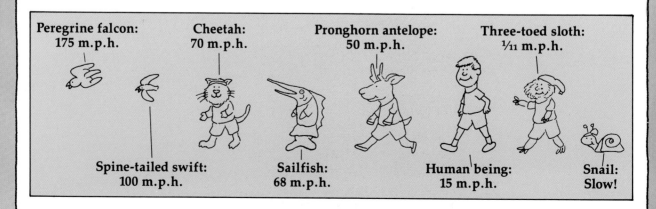

Peregrine falcon: 175 m.p.h.
Spine-tailed swift: 100 m.p.h.
Cheetah: 70 m.p.h.
Sailfish: 68 m.p.h.
Pronghorn antelope: 50 m.p.h.
Three-toed sloth: $\frac{1}{11}$ m.p.h.
Human being: 15 m.p.h.
Snail: Slow!

WHO'S THE SMALLEST?

The smallest mammal is *SAVI'S PYGMY SHREW*. It isn't much longer than 2 inches from the tip of its nose to the end of its tail. A pygmy shrew weighs less than a dime, but for its size it has the biggest appetite of any animal. It eats its own weight in food every three hours. Can you imagine what would happen if *you* did that?

The *BEE HUMMINGBIRD* from Cuba is the smallest bird. It is not much bigger than a bumblebee. Its nest is about the size of a thimble. This tiny hummingbird is a fantastic flier. It can move sideways or up and down—just like a helicopter. For food it drinks nectar from flowers.

The smallest reptile is the tiny *GECKO LIZARD*. It is only about 1½ inches long, but it is the noisiest lizard in the world. It chirps, squeaks, barks, and clicks to other geckos nearby. Using hooklike hairs, it also walks on walls and upside down on ceilings.

The colorless *DWARF PYGMY GOBY* is the smallest fish in the world. If you put 15,000 of them on a scale, they would weigh no more than a pound!

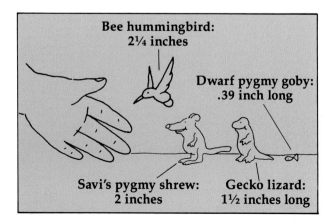

Bee hummingbird: 2¼ inches

Dwarf pygmy goby: .39 inch long

Savi's pygmy shrew: 2 inches

Gecko lizard: 1½ inches long

18

WHO'S THE BIGGEST?

The *AFRICAN ELEPHANT* is the largest land animal. The biggest one on record weighed as much as 16 cars—or 200 people. Elephants also have the longest teeth and noses. We call their long noses trunks. Their two tusks—which can be 11 feet long—are really overgrown front teeth.

The biggest bird is the *OSTRICH*. It often grows to a height of 9 feet. Though ostriches are birds, they cannot fly. They have small, useless wings. Since some of these giant birds weigh as much as two people, they would need extra strong wings to get into the air.

The heaviest insect is the *GOLIATH BEETLE* of Africa, which weighs as much as a small apple. It grows to a length of 4½ inches, has horns on its head, and can fly. Its hard, thick outer shell is like armor. Goliath beetles have been known to crash right through a windowpane!

The biggest animal that ever lived is still alive today—the female *BLUE WHALE*. Blue whales can weigh as much as 20 elephants (more than 286,000 pounds). They have hearts about the size of a small car. Though whales live and swim in the ocean, they are mammals—not fish. For food they eat tiny, shrimplike creatures called krill.

The biggest fish is the *WHALE SHARK*. It can grow as long as 60 feet and weigh as much as 22 tons. There are about 3,000 tiny teeth in its huge mouth, but the whale shark is a gentle, friendly giant. It eats only little fish and other small ocean creatures. Underwater divers have actually walked on its back.

The largest reptile is the *SALTWATER CROCODILE*. It can grow as long as 30 feet, and snap its huge jaws shut with the force of a 13-ton truck. However, the muscles that *open* its jaws are very weak. A person could hold them shut with one hand.

How the Rhinoceros Got His Skin

A Retelling of the Story by Rudyard Kipling

Once upon a time, long, long ago, on an island in the middle of the Red Sea, there lived a man from India. This man lived all alone on the island with nothing but a knife, a magical cookstove, and a brimless red hat.

One fine day, the Indian mixed up cake flour, currants, plums, and sugar. The cake pan measured two feet across and stood three feet high. Then he put it on his cookstove and watched it bake. Soon it was golden brown and smelled like nothing he had ever smelled before.

Just as he was about to cut the cake, a huge rhinoceros came lumbering down the beach, drawn by the smell of the cake, no doubt. The rhinoceros, who had no manners at all, stopped right in front of the cookstove with the delicious-smelling plum cake on top. He didn't say so much as a simple "hello" to the Indian.

The Indian stared at the enormous beast. In those days, the rhinoceros's skin fit him very tightly, which made him look as big as a house and twice as scary. He had two piggy eyes and a big horn on his nose that made him even more frightening.

"I want that cake!" said the rhinoceros to the Indian. And with that, the Indian forgot all about his delicious-smelling cake and climbed as fast as his legs could carry him up to the tippity-top of the nearest palm tree.

"Good," said the rhinoceros, thinking the cake was all his. With that, the rhinoceros kicked over the stove with his big foot, which set the plum cake rolling on the sand. Then he spiked the cake on the horn of his nose and slurped and gobbled it down as fast as he could.

"Delicious," he said, looking up at the Indian. Then he went away, waving his tail behind him.

As soon as the rhinoceros disappeared, the Indian climbed down from the tree. He was as mad as a hornet. He stomped around the empty cookstove and muttered over and over:

"Them that takes cakes
    which the island man bakes
    makes dreadful mistakes!"

And he shook his fist after that rude and mannerless rhinoceros and vowed to get even.

Now as it happened, there was a heat wave in the Red Sea a few weeks later. The Indian sat down by the sea and removed his red hat to cool off.

Soon, along came the very same giant rhinoceros that had eaten the Indian's plum cake. The rhinoceros looked at the Indian but said nothing about eating the cake. This rhinoceros had no manners at all. Then, without even a "How do you do?" the rhinoceros took off his skin and dove into the Red Sea. He waddled straight into the middle of the sea, then blew bubbles through his nose.

25

All the while, the Indian sat on the shore and watched the rhinoceros but said nothing. Suddenly, he smiled a smile that ran all around his face two times. He ran back to camp as fast as his legs would go, and swept up as many cake crumbs as he could find. The Indian never ate anything but cake and, since he never cleaned his campsite, it was full of crumbs. Carrying the crumbs in a sack, he ran back to the shore of the Red Sea and filled the rhinoceros's skin with as many crumbs as it would hold. Then he left it on the shore. "What fun!" he thought, climbing up a palm tree to wait. No sooner had the Indian climbed up the palm tree when the rhinoceros waded out of the water. He shook himself once, then slipped back into his skin. Suddenly that skin, which

26

had always fit so snugly and comfortably, tickled like cracker crumbs in bed.

The rhinoceros twitched and wiggled and wiggled and twitched. Those crumbs tickled him something terrible. He ran to a palm tree and rubbed, and rubbed, and rubbed. Soon he had rubbed so much that he rubbed his skin into a great fold over his shoulders, and another one underneath. The longer he rubbed, the more folds appeared. There were folds over his belly and folds on his legs and folds all over his back. And the more he rubbed, the more irritated he got. But it made no difference. So he went home very angry indeed, and horribly scratchy. And from that day to this, every rhinoceros has great folds of skin and a very bad temper.

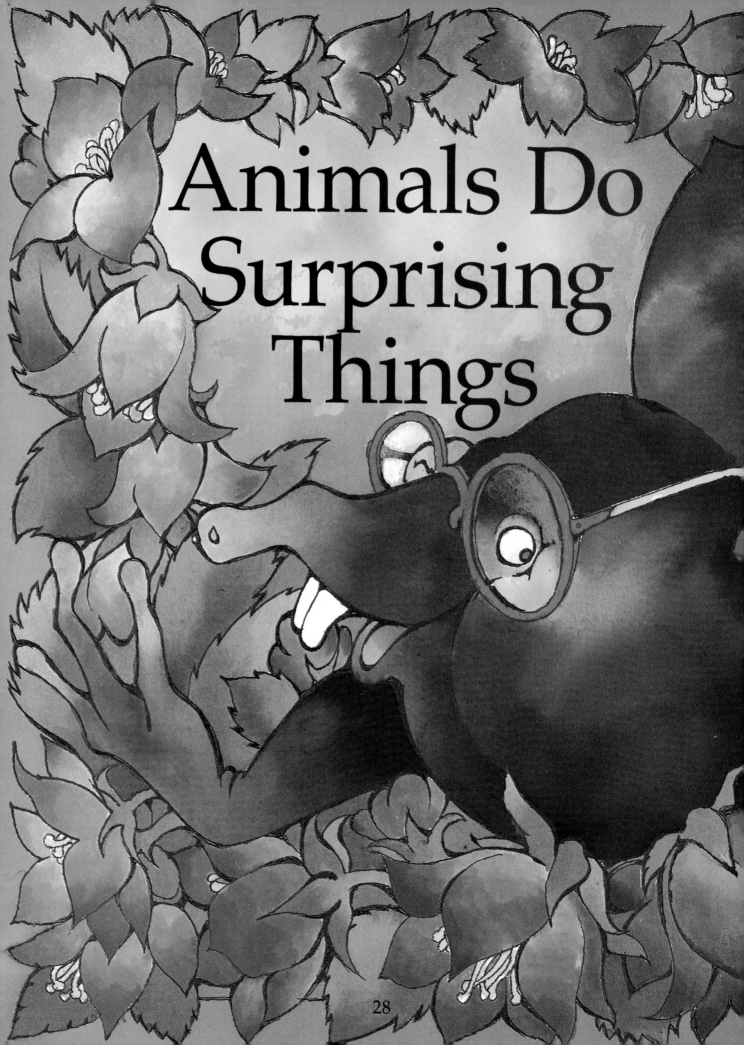

Animals Do
Surprising
Things

Mole

Jiminy Jiminy Jukebox! Wheatcakes! Crumbs!
Blow the bugle! Roll the drums!
Hide beneath the delphiniums!

Trim my whiskers! Bless my soul!
Here comes a big brown one-eyed Mole
All wound up like a jelly roll,
Too fat to waddle back to his hole!

Jiminy Jiminy Jukebox! Wheatcakes! Crumbs!

Howling Hatpin!

Here

he

comes!

William Jay Smith

29

ASTONISHING ANIMAL PARENTS

DID YOU KNOW...

...that **SEAHORSE** fathers hatch eggs? The mother deposits her eggs in a pouch on the father's stomach. The eggs hatch after a few weeks, and the father presses them out of the pouch. Though seahorses are fish, they are poor swimmers. They curl their tails around seaweed so that strong currents won't sweep them away.

...that **GREEN TURTLES** can swim over 1,400 miles? When it is time to lay their eggs, they swim across the Atlantic Ocean to the same beaches where they were born. When they arrive, the female turtles scoop out holes on sandy beaches and lay their eggs—often hundreds of them. They carefully cover the eggs with sand, then swim away again. Two or three months later, baby turtles dig their way out of the sandy nests, heading straight for the water. Off they swim, never having had a glimpse of their mothers.

...that the **OCEAN SUNFISH** lays more eggs than any other animal? It has been known to lay as many as 300 million! This peculiar-looking fish looks as if someone had cut off its back half. It has scarcely any tail fin at all. Full-grown, it can be 11 feet long and weigh a ton or more.

...that when they nest, **GREAT HORNBILLS** seal themselves into holes in trees? The female fills the hole by using her own droppings mixed with mud as a kind of plaster. (In some species, the male does this.) She lays her eggs and stays in the nest until the chicks are half-grown—from 6 to 12 weeks. The male feeds her and the chicks through a slit in the "plaster." Scientists think the hornbills developed this unusual way of nesting in order to keep monkeys from eating the eggs or the chicks.

...that **EMPEROR PENGUINS** hold their eggs on their feet through the Antarctic winter? The female lays a single egg. Then she dives into the water and swims away. The male stays behind and balances the egg on top of his feet, covering it with part of his body to keep it warm. For at least two long months, he stays very still—sometimes covered with snow—never eating, never moving. When spring comes, the chick hatches and the female returns, full of food to nourish the baby penguin. The male swims off for food, but he will return soon to help take care of the chick.

...that a baby **HIPPOPOTAMUS** is born underwater? It nurses underwater, too. The mother sometimes carries the baby on her back until it is able to swim. When a hippo mother wants to go off for any reason, she first finds a baby-sitter. Each group of hippos has a central nursery where females and young gather. There the mother leaves her calf with another female.

HUNTERS WITH STRANGE TASTES

DID YOU KNOW...

...that the **GIANT ANTEATER** has no teeth? It has something better—a tongue that is nearly 2 feet long! The anteater tears into anthills with its powerful front claws. Then it pokes its long, sticky tongue around the nest until the tongue is covered with ants. An anteater may eat thousands of ants or termites in just one meal.

...that a **CHIMPANZEE** uses tools to get termites? It takes a carefully chosen twig, pushes it into the termites' nest, and twists it around. When the chimp pulls the stick out, it is covered with termites. The clever chimp licks them off the stick, then pushes it back into the nest for a second helping. Nobody has figured out how the chimp gets the termites to stay on the twig.

...that the **ADDAX** never drinks water? The addax is a kind of horned antelope that lives in the North African desert. It gets all the liquid it needs from the plants that it eats.

...that **BEE EATERS** can eat bees without getting stung? Although these birds eat many kinds of insects, at least half of them are bees or wasps. To avoid getting stung, the bird bangs the bee on the head several times. Then it squeezes out the poison by rubbing the bee's stinging end against a branch. Bee eaters are friendly to each other. They hunt and live in small teams, and they are among the few birds that nest in tunnels built into cliff walls and dirt banks.

...that the **STARFISH** is not a fish? It's a spiny-skinned sea animal that lives along the shore. Its mouth and stomach are on the underside of its disk-shaped body. The body has five or more strong arms stretching out. The starfish uses these arms to grab and open mollusk shells. Then it pushes its stomach and mouth inside the shell to swallow and digest the soft animal living inside.

...that the **TRAP-DOOR SPIDER** has an unusual way of catching its dinner? It makes a tiny burrow or tunnel in the ground to hide in. Then it covers the entrance with a fine silk web hidden by moss or sand. When insects walk by, the spider opens the "door" and grabs them!

PECULIAR PROTECTION

DID YOU KNOW...

...that a **STRIPED SKUNK** sprays its enemies with a smelly liquid when threatened? First it turns its back. Then it raises its bushy tail, stamps its front feet, and growls. If the foolish enemy insists on coming closer, the skunk squirts a terrible-smelling liquid from two openings under its tail. It can even hit an animal that is 12 or 15 feet away.

...that **PORCUPINES** also turn their backs when attacked? A porcupine's upper side is covered with barbed quills. If an enemy comes too close, the porcupine raises its quills and lashes its tail. If the attacker actually touches the porcupine, the barbed quills will come out, burying themselves in the enemy's face or paws. They are painful and very difficult to remove.

. . . that the **OPOSSUM** protects itself by rolling over and playing dead? Its tongue hangs out and its eyes look glassy. As soon as the danger is over, the playacting opossum comes back to life.

...that the **FAIRY**—or *three-banded*—**ARMADILLO** travels in its own suit of armor? Its back, sides, head, and tail are all covered by bony plates. If an enemy attacks, the armadillo can just roll up into a hard little ball.

...that the **OCTOPUS** carries its own hiding place with it? When threatened by ocean-dwelling enemies, it simply squirts out a cloud of inklike fluid. This hides the octopus completely.

...that an **ELECTRIC EEL** carries its own supply of electricity? Rows and rows of small, natural battery cells inside its body can produce enough electricity to kill a person—or most enemies— on contact. This amazing fish could supply enough current to turn on a TV, a record player, a hair dryer, and a couple of light bulbs. However, they wouldn't *run* very long!

35

The Buffalo and the Egret
by Wendy Wax

There was once a big, brown buffalo who spent his days grazing in grassy fields and lazing in the hot sun. When he was hungry, he'd munch on grass and herbs. And when he was thirsty, he'd slurp water from a small pond. Night after night, the buffalo would look up at the star-filled sky and make a wish on the same blinking star. His wish was that he'd never meet up with a lion. Lions meant *trouble!*

In the same grassy fields, there lived a flock of egrets. All day long, the small white birds took turns hopping over one another, stirring up the soil, making insects spring up from the ground. The egrets would snap at the bugs with their beaks and gobble them up. And every once in a while, an egret would catch a grasshopper—a very special treat. (Egrets think grasshoppers are very, *very* tasty.)

Every egret in the flock had tried grasshopper at one time or another. That is, everyone except for the tiniest bird of the flock. This small egret always got pushed aside by the bigger egrets whenever there was a grasshopper around.

Night after night, the tiny white egret would look up at the star-filled sky and make a wish on the same blinking star. Her wish was that someday she'd get to taste a grasshopper.

One day, while the small egret was looking for some bugs for dinner, she heard a loud, thundering noise that shook the ground. The other egrets heard it, too, and fluttered away. But the poor tiny egret was too frightened to fly. So she hid in a cluster of yellow and white flowers.

The noise had been made by the buffalo, who was stomping his way to his favorite little pond. Once the buffalo had passed, the egret came out of hiding and found herself in a cloud of dust, feathers, and bugs that had been stirred up by the buffalo's hooves.

There were more tasty insects than the egret had ever seen before. And there was even a grasshopper! But before she could gobble up the grasshopper, it hopped off after the buffalo. So the egret followed the grasshopper.

The buffalo soon reached the pond. He nodded greetings to the zebras, tall giraffes, and the big, slow elephants. But instead of nodding back, they all stared at the buffalo's hooves. The buffalo wondered what they were all staring at, so he looked down. And there, going around and around, were the hungry little egret and the grasshopper.

The buffalo was angry. Why was a silly little bird chasing a bug around the legs of such a big and important buffalo? He was wondering what to do to make the egret go away, when suddenly the grasshopper jumped onto the buffalo's back. The egret followed the grasshopper.

While the buffalo was trying to shake the bird and the bug off his back, the egret finally gobbled up the grasshopper. And mmmm, was it yummy! The egret was so full after her dinner that she fell asleep right on the buffalo's head.

The buffalo was feeling tired, too, and terribly thirsty. So he went to take a drink. He could see his reflection in the ripples of water. And he saw the tiny white egret sleeping on his head! This made him angrier than ever.

Just then, the egret woke up. At first, she didn't know where she was. She looked around at the feathery leaves above the lake and then at the water below. Then she turned around—and there was a mean-looking lion sneaking up behind the buffalo!

At first, the tiny egret was much too frightened to fly. Instead, she began jumping and jumping on the buffalo's head. Finally, her wings began to flutter and she began flying.

The buffalo thought the egret was only trying to bother him, but then she flew off his head toward the lion. He watched her fly away—and then *he* saw the lion.

Never had the buffalo run so fast! He ran off into the grassy fields, past clusters of yellow and white flowers, past flocks of birds that flew away as he approached, and past zebras, elephants, giraffes, and other buffalo. The tiny egret flew overhead, trying to keep up. When the animals saw the buffalo running, they all ran off, too. They knew that danger was near.

Finally, the buffalo slowed down and the tired egret landed on his back. They both needed rest. And for once, the buffalo was happy to have the egret on his back.

From that day on, the big, brown buffalo and the tiny, white egret were friends. Every day, the egret followed the buffalo's hooves and caught more grasshoppers than any of the other egrets could catch in a whole week. And whenever a lion was around, the egret warned the buffalo by dancing and jumping on his head. And then the two of them would run off together.

And night after night, the buffalo and the egret said thank-you to the same blinking star.

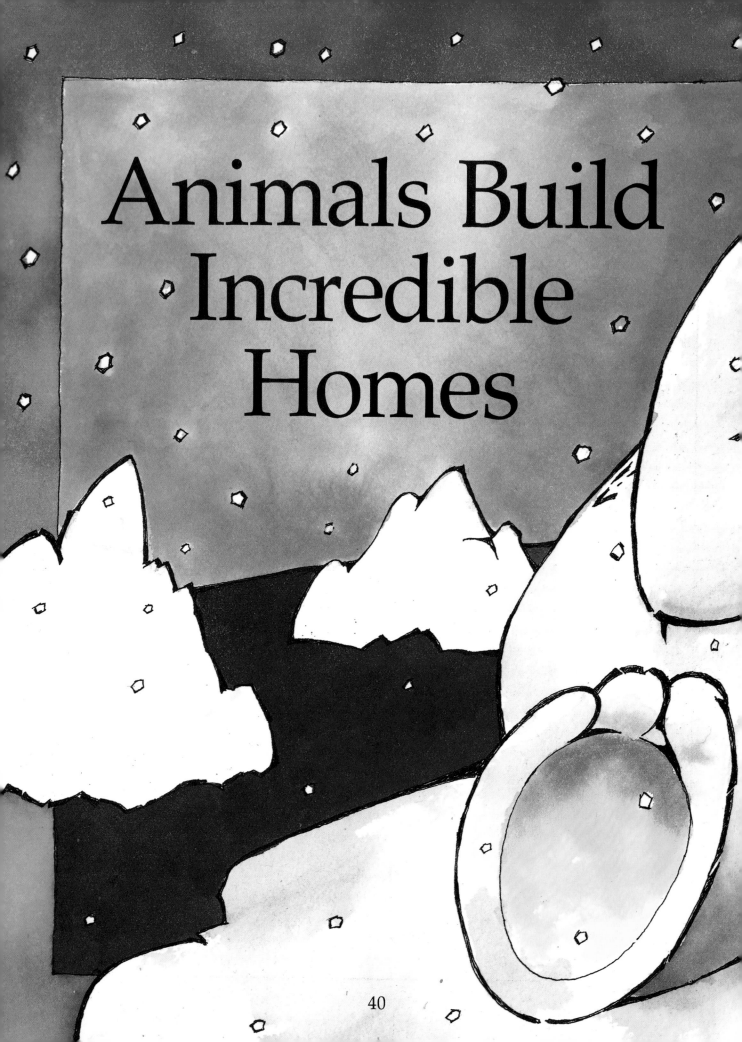

Animals Build Incredible Homes

Polar Bear

The Polar Bear never makes his bed;
He sleeps on a cake of ice instead.
He has no blanket, no quilt, no sheet
Except the rain and snow and sleet.
He drifts about on a white ice floe
While cold winds howl and blizzards blow
And the temperature drops to forty below.
The Polar Bear never makes his bed;
The blanket he pulls up over his head
Is lined with soft and feathery snow.
If ever he rose and turned out the light,
He would find a world of bathtub white,
And icebergs floating through the night.

William Jay Smith

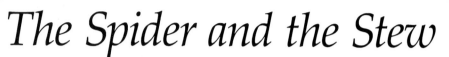

The Spider and the Stew

A Retelling of a Jamaican Folktale

N ow, some folks can't stand spiders. And some folks don't like stew. But this is a story about Anansi the Spider and his BIG, BIG appetite—especially for stew.

Anansi the Spider lived in his web in the jungle. He ate jungle flies and bumblebees and jungle fleas, which he caught in his web. But what he REALLY, REALLY wanted was stew. And it's pretty hard to catch stew in a spider web.

One day, Tiger came walking through the jungle on his way to the beach. "Morning, Anansi, care for a swim?" he called as he passed Anansi's web.

Anansi didn't like to swim, but he liked the aroma he was smelling. Tiger was carrying on his head a big pot of steaming stew—Anansi's favorite.

"Oh, I might come along for a swim," said Anansi, sniffing mightily. "But only if we go to a new spot. I know a place with a deep pool surrounded by high cliffs. It'll be fun!"

"It *looks* fun," said Tiger when they got there. "But it's awfully deep, Anansi. Are you sure you can swim here?"

"You will help me out if I can't do it myself," said Anansi. "You're a good friend, Tiger. And good friends share everything."

"Not this stew," said Tiger. "It's a special treat my wife made me. Will you watch it while I jump in and swim? I wouldn't want anyone to steal it."

"Oh, I'll watch it, dear Tiger," said the spider. "I'll watch it very, *very* closely."

So Tiger jumped in and splashed and swam, backward and forward and even underwater. Sometimes he looked up to see the stew pot sitting on the cliff. He waved at Anansi and kept on swimming.

Anansi got so hungry he could hardly stand it. Finally, while Tiger was diving down to touch the bottom of the river, Anansi emptied the stew onto a big leaf, which he gathered together like a pocket. And he gulped the stew down, every last drop. When Tiger next looked up, the stew pot was back on the cliff where it belonged—but this time it was empty.

"Come in, Anansi. The water's great!" called Tiger. "I'll come out and eat my stew."

"I've changed my mind. I don't care to swim today," said Anansi, and he hurried away. Tiger could be a good friend, but he could also be mad as a hornet when he was hungry.

Anansi swung through the jungle on his spider strings while he thought up a plan. All that good stew was helping him think.

Anansi went straight to Big Monkey Tree, where the biggest monkeys in the jungle spend their days.

"Monkeys, gather around, because I have a new song to make you clap your paws!" sang Anansi.

44

The monkeys loved songs, so they gathered around. And Anansi sang to them:

"I just finished Tiger's stew,
 Tiger's stew, Tiger's stew,
 I just finished Tiger's stew,
 But Tiger didn't see me."

The monkeys started dancing. (Monkeys always like a party!)
Soon all the monkeys were singing Anansi's new song.

"I just finished Tiger's stew,
 Tiger's stew, Tiger's stew,
 I just finished Tiger's stew,
 But Tiger didn't see me."

45

They swung and clapped and threw each other up in the air as they sang. It was a sight to see. When monkeys have a party, it lasts a long time. Anansi is a clever spider. He knows these things.

Anansi crept away into the jungle until he found Tiger, who was asking every creature he met who had eaten his lovely stew.

"I think I know!" said Anansi. "We're good friends, and we share everything. So let me take you to Big Monkey Tree, and you will see what you will see!"

Anansi and Tiger went back to Big Monkey Tree. There Tiger heard the monkeys singing and dancing.

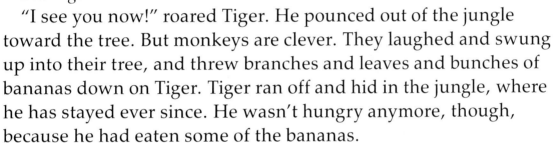

"I just finished Tiger's stew,
Tiger's stew, Tiger's stew,
I just finished Tiger's stew,
But Tiger didn't see me."

"I see you now!" roared Tiger. He pounced out of the jungle toward the tree. But monkeys are clever. They laughed and swung up into their tree, and threw branches and leaves and bunches of bananas down on Tiger. Tiger ran off and hid in the jungle, where he has stayed ever since. He wasn't hungry anymore, though, because he had eaten some of the bananas.

And Anansi climbed back into his safe, high web and fell asleep, dreaming of a whole deep river of lovely stew!

THE ARCTIC

Many animals live in the Arctic, the snow- and ice-covered land around the North Pole. Can you find the 14 animals shown below? They are all hidden in this picture.

Arctic fox

Bearded seal

Arctic tern

Ivory gull

Polar bear

Puffin

Harp seal

Musk ox

Hooded seal

Lapland bunting

Lemming

Arctic hare

Walrus

Reindeer

THE RAIN FOREST

Some of the most amazing animals live in rain forests and jungles. The 16 shown below are all hidden in this picture. Can you find them?

Amazon river dolphin

Hatchetfish

Morpho butterfly

Spider monkey

Scarlet macaw

Quetzal

Anaconda snake

Giant anteater

Emerald tree boa

Toucan

Capybara

Nine-banded armadillo

Ocelot

Sloth

Pygmy marmoset

Ruby topaz hummingbird

THE DESERT

There are many interesting animals that live in the hot, dry desert. In this desert picture, can you find all 15 of the animals shown below?

Tree lizard

Gila monster

Badger

Western spadefoot frog

Elf owl

Mountain lion

Roadrunner

Desert tortoise

Peccary

Kangaroo rat

Tarantula

Sidewinder snake

Mule deer

Kit fox

Jackrabbit

A CLOSER LOOK:
ANIMAL HOUSES

BEAVERS are very clever builders. They can cut down whole trees with their four sharp front teeth. They float the trees downstream to build dams across streams and rivers. Then they pile the logs on top of each other and fill in the holes with mud and stones. The dam holds back the water, making a pond or lake.

After the dam is finished, the beavers build a round lodge in the pond. For this they use sticks stuck together with more mud. The living space in the lodge is above water, but the tunnels leading to it are underwater. The tunnels protect the beavers from enemies. Beavers often work together in large family groups. One huge beaver pond in New Hampshire contained 40 lodges that had been built over the years.

Beavers like water. Their big hind feet are webbed for swimming, and their thick coat of fur is waterproofed with oil. A beaver can stay underwater for as long as 15 minutes.

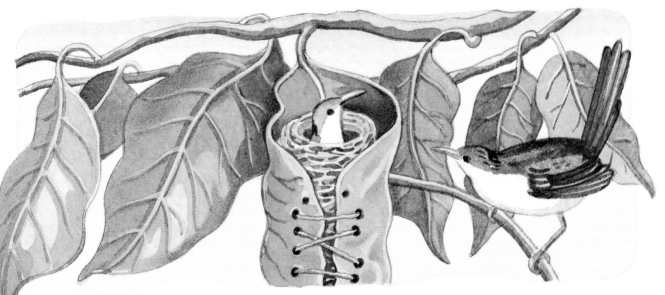

Some birds build amazing homes, too. The **LONG-TAILED TAILORBIRD** uses its beak as a needle to sew together the edges of one or two large leaves. This makes a kind of funnel-shaped bag for the outside of its nest. For thread the tailorbird finds silk from spiderwebs, cotton fibers, and string. It pierces holes along the edge of the leaves and draws the "thread" through with its beak. Each time it pulls the thread through the hole, it makes a knot on the outside so the thread can't slip back. It lines the nest with fine grasses and animal hairs.

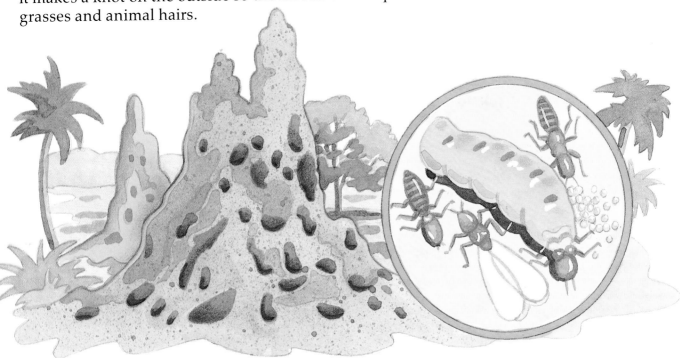

The tallest insect homes are those built by **TERMITE** colonies in Africa and Australia. These termites build high towers of mud cemented with their saliva. Inside the tower there is a whole system of tunnels and rooms. The tunnels, which begin below ground, are arranged in a way that produces a perfect air-conditioning system. Termite mounds more than 20 feet tall have been found in Africa. The outer crust of the tower is so hard that a person would need a steel pick to break through it. Sometimes as many as 10 million termites—including queen, soldiers, and workers—live together in one colony.

THE TOWNS THAT "DOGS" BUILD

Some of the most amazing animal homes are the *towns* built by **PRAIRIE DOGS.** Actually, prairie dogs are not dogs at all. They are rodents, as are squirrels and mice and beavers. Like other rodents, they have four chisel-shaped, sharp front teeth for gnawing. Prairie dogs got their unusual name because they live on prairies in the southwestern United States and often make a barking noise like a dog.

Prairie dogs make their homes in burrows or tunnels that they dig underground. The entrance goes straight down for several feet. Then it levels off into a tunnel. Different "rooms" open off the tunnels. There is usually a room to nest in, a room for storing food, and a small room near the opening to serve as a listening post. The prairie dogs also pack mounds of dirt around the entrance to their burrows. This helps to keep out rain and enemies. Badgers, foxes, ferrets, and cats all hunt prairie dogs. So do eagles and hawks. The burrows are guarded outside by sentries who give the alarm with a series of whistling barks if they spot an enemy. There are different calls to indicate whether the enemy is coming by land or from the air.

A prairie dog family is a very close unit. Prairie dogs groom each other, hug and kiss, and play together. A family is called a *coterie*. When young family members grow into adults, they build new burrows next door. These areas are called *territories*. Gradually the territories extend for miles and miles in every direction. They are called prairie dog *towns*. Long ago, one of these towns was found in Texas containing about 400 million animals. It covered an area that was more than three times the size of the state of New Jersey! Today the biggest towns cover only 200 or 300 acres.

This is what a part of a prairie dog home looks like. Can you see the mounds of dirt around the entrance? A prairie dog is in the room used as a listening post. Two more prairie dogs are in a room with a nice, warm nest in it.

The Snake That Came to Spend the Winter

by Michael Pellowski

![W]inter is a long, lonely time," said Gomer Gopher to his friends Matilda Mole and Melissa Mouse. "Sometimes you end up trapped in your burrow for months with no one to talk to. And *I* like to *talk*."

Matilda Mole smiled and winked at Melissa Mouse. They both knew just how much Gomer liked to talk. He was always talking! Gomer didn't even care if anyone was really listening to what he had to say. He just liked to babble on and on. The little gopher chattered so much, all of his friends called him Gabby.

"Why don't you get a roommate?" suggested Melissa. Melissa and Matilda were roommates, and they got along together very well.

"I would love a roommate! Then I could talk late into the night. I could stay up late and chat and talk for hours on end! We could talk until morning! There are so many things I would want to talk about!"

Matilda and Melissa shook their heads. "There isn't a roommate in the world who could do that. They would want to sleep," they both said.

"I know," replied Gabby. "That's why I live alone. And that is why winter is a long and lonely time for me. There is no perfect roommate for me!" Gabby waved to his friends and bounded off toward his cozy burrow. Gabby's home was all ready for winter. His burrow was lined with comfy straw, and his storeroom was crammed full of food. The little gopher happily slipped through the tunnel leading to his home and dropped down into his living room.

"Ga-aah!" gasped Gabby as he glanced around. He backed up against the wall in alarm. Dozing in the warmest corner of his burrow was Sidney Snake!

"Who invited *you*?" Gabby sputtered. "What are you doing here?"

Sidney didn't answer. He just continued to snooze peacefully. He was beginning his winter hibernation.

"I've heard that since snakes can't dig their own burrows, they sometimes move into other animals' homes," babbled Gabby. "So you're perfectly welcome here. I've always wanted a roommate! How long do you want to stay? What do you like to talk about? I'll talk about anything! Anything at all!"

Sidney slowly opened one eye. His tail twitched just a little. "Please be quiet," he slowly said, hissing. "Can't you see I'm trying to sleep?"

60

"I've always meant to ask you why you sleep all winter," Gabby said, talking faster and faster. "Why would anybody want to sleep for such a long time when there's so much to do? But I'm just happy you're here. I love having someone to talk to!"

"Please, oh please..." hissed Sidney quietly. He was very tired, and wanted to get some rest.

But Gabby just kept on going. "We're having alfalfa salad and acorn stew for dinner," Gabby shouted. Sidney only wiggled a bit. He hoped Gabby would stop talking for a while. If only Sidney could get just a little sleep! He closed his eyes...

CRASH! Gabby had dragged out a giant pot and was filling it with acorns, yackity-yacking all the while. BOOM! He started filling a huge bowl with salad. Sidney just stayed in his corner.

"Isn't this a nice house? It's so warm and comfy. You're not eating! Aren't you hungry? Or maybe you would like something else?" Gabby had started talking and wouldn't stop.

On and on Gabby talked, long into the night. Not once did Sidney Snake disagree or interrupt. He just remained very quiet. That made Gabby Gopher very happy. "I think we're going to get along fine during the winter," Gabby said to Sidney. "Having a snake as a roommate might not be so bad after all."

All winter long, Gabby chattered and talked and babbled. He never really noticed that Sidney never said anything in return. But that didn't bother Gabby at all. In fact, the little gopher was very happy. He wasn't the least bit lonely during the long, cold months of winter snow and ice.

One day, when spring had finally come, Sidney Snake's tail slowly twitched. Gabby was still talking, and didn't even notice that Sidney was moving around. Sidney opened his eyes. "Good morning," he hissed.

"What do you mean, 'good morning'? It was morning *hours* ago. Didn't you notice?" Gabby babbled.

"Of course not," said Sidney. "I was having the *most* delightful sleep! You are the *perfect* host!"

For once, Gabby didn't know what to say. All this time, he had been talking, but Sidney hadn't heard a thing! Only then did Gabby realize that his roommate had been *hibernating*. He had slept all through winter! And Gabby hadn't felt lonely at all. Sidney Snake was the perfect roommate!

As Sidney slowly made his way outside, Gabby called after him, "Come back again next winter if you like. This time, you're invited!"

Little People™ Big Book About THE ANIMAL KINGDOM

TIME-LIFE for CHILDREN™

Publisher: Robert H. Smith
Managing Editor: Neil Kagan
Associate Editors: Jean Burke Crawford,
        Patricia Daniels
Marketing Director: Ruth P. Stevens
Promotion Director: Kathleen B. Tresnak
Associate Promotion Director: Jane B. Welihozkiy
Production Manager: Prudence G. Harris
Editorial Consultants: Jacqueline A. Ball, Sara Mark

PRODUCED BY PARACHUTE PRESS, INC.

Editorial Director: Joan Waricha
Editors: Christopher Medina, Jane Stine, Wendy Wax
Writers: Gregory Maguire, Walter Retan, Michael
        Pellowski, Jean Waricha, Wendy Wax
Designer: Deborah Michel
Illustrators: Yvette Banek (p. 12), Diane DeGroat (p. 6),
        Pat & Robin DeWitt (pp. 48-53), Jeff
        DiNardo (pp. 16-21), Robert Frank (p. 10),
        Janice Fried (pp. 14-15), Marti Shohet (pp.
        56-57), John Speirs (cover, pp. 4-5, 28-29,
        36-39, 40-41), John Wallner (pp. 22-27)

Time-Life Books Inc. is a wholly owned subsidiary
of THE TIME INC. BOOK COMPANY.

TIME-LIFE is a trademark of Time Warner Inc. U.S.A.

FISHER-PRICE, LITTLE PEOPLE and AWNING
DESIGN are trademarks of Fisher-Price, Division of
The Quaker Oats Company, and are used under
license.

Time-Life Books Inc. offers a wide range of fine
publications, including home video products. For
subscription information, call 1-800-621-7026, or
write TIME-LIFE BOOKS, P.O. Box C-32068, Rich-
mond, Virginia 23261-2068.

ACKNOWLEDGMENTS

Every effort has been made to trace the ownership of all copyrighted material and to secure the necessary
permissions to reprint these selections. If any question arises as to the use of any material, the editor and the
publisher, while expressing regret for any inadvertent error, will make the necessary correction in future
printings.

Grateful acknowledgment is made to the following for permission to reprint copyrighted material: Farrar, Straus
& Giroux for "Mole" and "Polar Bear" from LAUGHING TIME by William Jay Smith. Copyright © 1955, 1957,
1980, 1990 by William Jay Smith. Gina Maccoby Literary Agency for "Elephant" from THE RAUCOUS AUK: A
MENAGERIE OF POEMS by Mary Ann Hoberman. Copyright © 1973 by Mary Ann Hoberman. Random House,
Inc. for "The Yak" by Jack Prelutsky, from THE RANDOM HOUSE BOOK OF POETRY FOR CHILDREN,
selected and introduced by Jack Prelutsky. Copyright © 1983 by Random House, Inc.

TIME-LIFE BOOKS
ALEXANDRIA, VIRGINIA

Leap and Dance

The lion walks on padded paws,
The squirrel leaps from limb to limb,
While flies can crawl straight up a wall,
And seals can dive and swim.
The worm, it wiggles all around,
The monkey swings by its tail,
And birds may hop upon the ground,
Or spread their wings and sail.
But boys and girls have much more fun;
 They leap and dance
 And walk
 And *run*.

Anonymous